DOGS AT WORK

DOGS AT WORK

BY JAMES McCLOY

ILLUSTRATED BY SHEILA BEATTY

CROWN PUBLISHERS, INC.
NEW YORK

To all my family

Text copyright © 1979 by James McCloy
Illustrations copyright © 1979 by Sheila Beatty
All rights reserved. No part of this publication may be reproduced, stored in a retrieval system, or transmitted, in any form or by any means, electronic, mechanical, photocopying, recording, or otherwise, without prior written permission of the publisher. Inquiries should be addressed to Crown Publishers, Inc., One Park Avenue, New York, N.Y. 10016. Manufactured in the United States of America. Published simultaneously in Canada by General Publishing Company Limited.

10   9   8   7   6   5   4   3   2   1

The text of this book is set in 14 point Melior.
The illustrations are pencil drawings reproduced in halftone.

Library of Congress Cataloging in Publication Data
McCloy, James   Dogs at work.   Summary: "Introduces eleven breeds of dogs that have worked for people in the past and that continue to be used in different but equally important ways." 1. Working dogs —Juvenile literature. 2. Dog breeds—Juvenile literature. [1. Working dogs. 2. Dog breeds] I. Beatty, Sheila. II. Title.   SF428.2.M32   636.73   78-24558   ISBN 0-517-53408-8

CONTENTS

INTRODUCTION

Today most of us think of dogs as pets. But in the past survival was difficult, and pets were a luxury few people could afford. Dogs had to be helpful in some way, and even today many dogs still work hard for people.

The common ancestor of all dogs was most probably the wolf. In ancient times wolves followed people and ate the food they left behind. When wolves killed an animal, people sometimes drove the wolves away and ate the food themselves.

Possibly as a result of the people breeding the wolves that lived near them, and because of changes in size, shape, and color that no one has been able to explain, some wolves gradually evolved into the animals we think of as dogs. Scientists believe that dogs and people have lived together for over twelve thousand years.

People learned that dogs possess better senses of smell and hearing, and can run faster than people. In both dogs and people the nerve cells that detect odors are in a membrane in the nasal passages. Dogs have many more of these cells than people and can therefore pick up scents too faint for our noses to detect. And because dogs have more highly developed nerve endings in their ears, they can hear sounds which we cannot hear at all.

When people discovered that dogs had these natural abilities, they trained them to do many kinds of work. Dogs helped people hunt other animals for food, and they guarded the people's homes. When people began to raise sheep and cattle for food and clothing, dogs were trained to keep the herds together and to protect them from wild animals.

People selected dogs that were especially suited to certain jobs and bred them to produce offspring that were even better at these jobs. Breeding dogs for special abilities is called selective breeding. It is an extremely complicated procedure, but in simple terms it works in the following way.

When any two dogs mate, the litter of puppies will have a combination of the parents' skills and looks. When a specific quality is desired—for example, a keen sense of smell—the mating of the dogs must be carefully controlled.

By mating dogs with a keen sense of smell, there is a much better chance that one or more of their puppies will have this quality. Those puppies can then be singled out and mated. If this is done for several generations, the number of puppies born in each litter with a keen sense of smell will gradually increase. Eventually each litter will consist of only dogs with this quality. Dogs with the same ability can be bred to produce that ability; or dogs with different abilities can be bred to produce dogs with all of those abilities.

Hunters bred dogs that could smell or see well. Sheepherders bred dogs that showed skill in controlling sheep. In time these abilities became inbred, or permanent, in different breeds of dogs. This is why the Bloodhound can follow a scent along the ground better than the Border Collie. On the other hand, the Border Collie is better at herding sheep than the Bloodhound.

People have bred dogs for thousands of years, but some types of dogs were developed later than others. As people bred these dogs for their special qualities, each kind of dog developed a distinctive appearance.

Long ago, day-to-day life was difficult. But dogs performed certain tasks for people that made their lives easier and more comfortable. This book introduces eleven breeds of dog that have worked for people in the past and that continue to be used in different but equally important ways.

GREAT PYRENEES

The Great Pyrenees (pronounced PEER-e-neez) is named for the Pyrenees Mountains, which lie along the border between France and Spain. In these mountains, where life is rugged, people have used this dog in many ways.

The Great Pyrenees is solidly built and may weigh as much as 125 pounds. Its long coat is either solid white or white with faint markings of gray, tan, or brown.

For centuries, the Great Pyrenees helped shepherds protect their flocks. Its herding instinct is so strong that a young Great Pyrenees may run in circles around sheep without having seen them before, or without having received special training. At one time the Great Pyrenees wore an iron collar with one-and-one-half-inch spikes on it. Protected by this collar and by its thick coat, the Great Pyrenees drove wolves and bears away from flocks of sheep.

Because the Great Pyrenees instinctively protects its master, it has often been used as a guard dog. In the past, many castles in France, including that of King Louis XIV, who reigned from 1643–1715, were protected by packs of these dogs. The Great Pyrenees stood guard with soldiers and barked when someone approached.

When the dog was not working, it usually slept on the doormat in front of its master's house. This is how it earned the nickname of "mat-dog."

The Great Pyrenees also sailed with fishermen, who used them to haul their nets out of the water. At times they were used for pulling carts filled with crops to market by farmers who couldn't afford horses. Some smugglers along the border between France and Spain strapped loads of goods to the Great Pyrenees's backs, and the dogs crossed the border on narrow mountain trails, undetected by the guards.

Today the Great Pyrenees is used by skiers to carry supplies and to draw sleds where cars cannot go. Because of its ability to smell the ground beneath the snow, the dog is able to warn skiers to stay away from areas where the snow isn't firmly packed. The dogs walk around the spot, and the skiers know to avoid it.

NEWFOUNDLAND

This breed was developed on the island of Newfoundland in Canada over two hundred and fifty years ago. The Newfoundland is probably a descendant of the Great Pyrenees, the English Retriever, and the other large breeds that were at one time carried on fishing boats. From these dogs the Newfoundland inherited its webbed feet. The web, a thin skin that stretches between the toes, results in a broad foot that the dog uses like a paddle. These feet make the Newfoundland an exceptionally fine swimmer.

The Newfoundland has a thick, coarse black coat that protects it from icy water. It is a large, powerful dog and may weigh up to 150 pounds.

In the 1800s and earlier, sailing ships often carried Newfoundlands. The Newfoundland was trained to jump into the water to rescue people who fell overboard. The dog would then return to the ship, pulling the person with its strong teeth, or with the person holding onto its back. The Newfoundland saved many people from drowning. One of these dogs rescued Napoleon in 1814.

The Newfoundland's use was not limited to rescuing people. Fishermen in Newfoundland used the dogs to pull their nets from the water and onto the land. They also hauled carts full of fish and other loads. By the early 1800s Newfoundlands helped people in many ways. When a ship became lodged on rocks near

the shore, a trained Newfoundland would swim to it with a rope. People on land then pulled on the rope, which had been tied to a lifeboat. The Newfoundland was also large enough and strong enough to haul lumber from the forests to the sawmills. And in some areas of Newfoundland, mailmen used the dogs to carry the mail. These dogs were so useful that some people were able to earn their living solely by owning them and renting them out.

While the Newfoundland still works with fishermen today, modern machinery is being used for most of the work.

Although the Newfoundland has been relied upon for its strength, it is a very gentle dog and makes a good pet. It allows young children to climb all over it, and because of its size, is not easily hurt.

BLOODHOUND

The Bloodhound has the most highly developed sense of smell of all the breeds. Over the years many different dogs with good senses of smell have been called bloodhounds, but today there is only one breed that is properly called the Bloodhound.

The Bloodhound's ancestors first appeared in the Middle East over two thousand years ago. During the Middle Ages in France, bishops bred these hounds for hunting. About one hundred thirty years ago the Bloodhound was brought to the United States from England, where it had been known since the 1400s. It is here that the dog now does most of its work.

The Bloodhound weighs between 80 and 110 pounds and has a short, hard coat that is either black and tan, reddish-brown and tan, or solid tan. Its name may come from the fact that many people of upper-class "blood" owned them for hunting. Or it may refer to the dog's ability to follow the smell of the blood from a wounded animal. Some people mistakenly believe that the dog's name means that it is bloodthirsty and vicious.

In the past, the Bloodhound was used both for hunting and for finding missing farm animals. More recently, however, the Bloodhound has been used for tracking criminals and lost people. Unlike the German Shepherd, the Bloodhound is not useful for any police work other than tracking. It is calm and friendly by nature and doesn't offer much protection to its owner. It is slower to learn than some breeds; it does not move quickly, and it is messy because it drools a lot. But no other dog can follow a scent as well.

When the Bloodhound is trained, it first sniffs an article of clothing that belongs to the person it is supposed to find. The trainer, who knows where this person is hidden, guides the Bloodhound on a leash along the trail left by that person. The

Bloodhound picks up the person's scent and follows it. It practices following scents for many months. The dog works best in the country because the cool, damp ground retains the scent of a person better than the cement and concrete of the city or hot, dry ground. It is not confused by the scents of other people and animals. It picks out the scent of the person it is supposed to follow and moves along the trail slowly but steadily. Since it is not an agile dog, the Bloodhound may have to be lifted over a log or a low fence so it can continue to follow the trail.

The Bloodhound can pick up a scent that is as much as five days old and follow it for a distance of up to 50 miles. A famous Bloodhound named Nick Carter lived in Kentucky during the 1930s and found over six hundred criminals and lost people.

Another dog, named Barney, lived in New Jersey, and by the time he died in 1977, he had found 377 people.

Most photographs of Bloodhounds show them on leashes, especially if they are with police who are following a suspect. If the Bloodhound were to reach the suspect first, the dog and the suspect might become friends and run off together.

Occasionally when the search is over, the Bloodhound falls asleep, and its trainer has to carry it back to the truck that picks them up. Stories like these make the Bloodhound seem a silly, slow-witted dog, but it's not.

Throughout the United States, Bloodhounds are used for tracking as often as six hundred times a year. But some days a Bloodhound just doesn't feel like working. It may yawn and lie down and refuse to go on the trail. When this happens, its trainers must use other Bloodhounds, or wait for another day.

BOUVIER DES FLANDRES

This dog's name comes from its work. Bouvier des Flandres (pronounced BOO-vee-ay day FLAWN-druh) is French for "cowherd of Flanders." For centuries these dogs were used to drive cattle in Flanders—the area of Belgium where the breed originated. It is now used elsewhere, including the United States.

Long ago, when people cooked over fires, Bouvier des Flandres were trained to run on treadmills. These treadmills turned

meat on a spit or stick that was placed over the fire, and the meat was cooked on all sides. For their hours of work, the dogs were rewarded with pieces of meat.

Until the early 1900s Bouvier des Flandres were a variety of shapes and sizes. Then breeders decided to breed dogs that were more uniform in appearance but still had the ability to herd cattle. During World War I, armies destroyed most of the farms in Belgium and France where these dogs were raised. The breeding was stopped, and the Bouvier des Flandres faced extinction. Luckily breeding began again after the war, and the number of these dogs grew rapidly.

The breeding produced a dog that is solidly built and can weigh as much as 110 pounds. The Bouvier des Flandres' coat is wiry and rough. It is usually fawn, black, gray, or salt and pepper, in color. The long hair on its face gives it the appearance of having a moustache and beard. For the sake of what breeders consider good looks, its tail is docked, or cut off, and its ears are cropped.

In order to move cattle, the Bouvier des Flandres is trained to push them with its shoulders and chest. Using this technique, the dog keeps the cattle tightly together while the farmer walks them along the road. Because the Bouvier des Flandres learns its job so well, it can be left to work alone.

In parts of rural Belgium and Holland, the Bouvier des Flandres was hitched to a little cart with milk cans in it. The dog pulled the cart as the farmer made his deliveries. If the farmer owned two Bouvier des Flandres, he could ride in the cart as well.

Because of advances in modern transportation, fewer dogs are used for delivering milk in this way. But as a guard dog, as a seeing-eye dog, and as a police dog, the Bouvier des Flandres works for us today.

DALMATIAN

The exact origin of the Dalmatian is not known, but it is believed that this breed evolved hundreds of years ago in a region of Yugoslavia called Dalmatia. The Dalmatian is noted for its striking appearance. It is a lean, short-haired dog, and its white coat is covered with many small black or brown spots. Dalmatian puppies are born pure white and only develop spots after they are several weeks old. When fully grown, the Dalmatian weighs about 55 pounds. Throughout history, the Dalmatian has been used as a shepherd, a hunter, a guard, and a pack dog. However, this dog has long been associated with traveling people. Because it lived in stables, it got along well with horses. For centuries it accompanied gypsy caravans around Europe.

In Europe during the 1700s, the Dalmatian was such a common sight on coaches that it was often called the "coach dog." Dalmatians were used to scare off bandits and to drive wolves away from the horses. When farm animals blocked the road, the Dalmatian herded them to one side so that the coach could continue its journey. Dalmatians became known for their great courage and for their agility. They were able to run alongside and underneath coaches and between the horses as well.

In the United States in the 1800s, many fire departments adopted Dalmatians as mascots because of their ability to get along with horses. Sometimes the Dalmatians rode on the horse-drawn fire engines; at other times they raced through the streets next to the horses.

When cars began to replace horses in the early 1900s, Dalmatians were no longer needed to escort coaches or fire engines. But because of their traditional role, Dalmatians are still seen in fire stations, and they ride on coaches in parades.

GERMAN SHEPHERD

The German Shepherd is one of the best-known dogs. There may be more German Shepherds in the world than any other single breed. The German Shepherd has served as a police dog, guard dog, and military dog. It has guided the blind, tended flocks of sheep, and has rescued people buried in avalanches in the Alps.

The German Shepherd is one of the newer breeds of dogs that work. For centuries shepherd dogs were different sizes and shapes because sheep owners were more interested in a dog's herding skills than in its appearance. But in the 1890s, in Germany, a man named Captain Max von Stephanitz decided to breed a dog that was uniform in its traits and physical appearance.

Von Stephanitz obtained a dog named Horand. Horand was strong, obedient, loyal, courageous, and intelligent; he looked much like the German Shepherd of today. This dog became the first member of the German Shepherd breed. Von Stephanitz bred Horand with other shepherd dogs that had the characteristics he desired. The German Shepherd that resulted weighs between 65 and 85 pounds and has a short, thick coat that is a mixture of black, tan, and gray.

The German Shepherd was an excellent sheepherder. But a number of factors—the growth of railroads, the fencing in of pastures, and the diminishing numbers of wild animals that might attack sheep—caused fewer dogs to be needed for this purpose. German Shepherds then came to be used for police work.

Almost all of the police dogs in the United States are German Shepherds. Dogs are selected for this work on the basis of their alertness, their intelligence, their agility, and their ability to learn—not for their viciousness.

The German Shepherd that is being trained for police work begins a fourteen-week course when it is from six to fourteen months old. The dog learns to obey its trainer. It also learns special skills it will need—such as climbing to high places and jumping through windows and over obstacles. Guns are fired near the dog so it will not be frightened of the noise.

The German Shepherd is sometimes trained to be a police attack dog. For this job, the dog receives special schooling. First an unfamiliar trainer wearing a thickly padded sleeve for protection teases the dog, which makes it mad. After a lot of teasing, the dog is allowed to sink its teeth into the sleeve. Following each attack, the trainer retreats. This leads the dog to believe it will always overpower an attacker. In police work, the German

Shepherd attacks only when commanded to or when its trainer is in trouble. When the dog attacks, it grabs the person's sleeve and twists it back and forth. This keeps the person off balance until help can arrive.

In addition to this police work, German Shepherds are now being taught to locate drugs and explosives by detecting their smell and to follow the trails of suspected criminals or lost people. Police in Israel and Australia have bred German Shepherds with Bloodhounds. They hope to develop a dog with the German Shepherd's strength and speed and the Bloodhound's more highly developed sense of smell.

Many German Shepherds are kept by private companies or by individuals as guard dogs. Their keen sense of smell and acute hearing enable them to lead a guard directly to an intruder. Some guard dogs even spend the night by themselves in stores or fenced-in areas. These German Shepherds are taught to accept food and water only from those people who feed and care for them. They won't accept food or water from anyone else, so it is impossible for an intruder to poison them.

They are locked in special kennels during the day, where people tease them to make them vicious. Warning signs are posted, and many intruders will not break into places they know are guarded by German Shepherds.

SAMOYED

This dog was named for the nomadic Samoyed people who live on the cold tundra of Sibera in northeastern Russia. In its native land it is hard to see this dog because its white coat blends with the snow. For hundreds of years the Samoyed has helped this people to herd reindeer; it has also carried packs on its back and has been used as a guard dog. In the late 1800s, the Samoyed was brought to Europe, and from there it was taken to North America.

The Samoyed usually weighs about 50 pounds. The dog's black lips contrast sharply with its pure white fur, and they curl up at the corners, causing it to look as if it is smiling. The Samoyed's fur stands straight out from its body; its bushy tail curls smartly over its back. This thick fur keeps the dog warm. In cold climates, the Samoyed digs a hole in the snow at night and rolls itself in a furry ball and goes to sleep. The Samoyed can spend days on end outside, even when the temperature is far below zero.

The Samoyed is best known as a sled dog. It has carried supplies and provided transportation for people in cold climates longer than any other breed. A sled team of Samoyeds consists of from seven to ten dogs. A dog is chosen to be a lead dog because of its intelligence and strength. While hitched to a sled, the lead dog learns to take commands from the driver—to turn right or left, to go faster, and to stop. The rest of the team is then taught to do what the lead dog does. When the lead dog runs faster, the other dogs run faster as well.

The team is hitched to a sled in one of three ways: in single file, in pairs, or in lines of equal length that spread out in a fanlike

formation. The dogs begin to run when they hear the driver shout. A driver and his team may travel 20 to 40 miles a day.

In the late 1800s and early 1900s, Samoyed teams were used by explorers near the North and South poles and by fur traders and prospectors in Alaska and Canada. Because people now use airplanes and snowmobiles, fewer sled teams are used today. But Samoyeds are occasionally used to rescue people from places where airplanes cannot land. A team of dogs, a driver, and a sled are dropped by parachute from an airplane to a point near the stranded people. At first the fall frightens the dogs, but they recover quickly and rally around their driver for the rescue.

The sport of racing Samoyeds and other sled dogs—the Siberian Husky, the Alaskan Malamute, and the Eskimo Dog, for instance—is popular today, especially in the United States and

Canada. The Samoyed is not the fastest sled dog, but it still competes well against the other breeds and in races limited to Samoyeds.

The Samoyed helps people in a way that doesn't seem like work. After the dog is combed, its loose hair is gathered up and spun into yarn in much the same way as sheep's wool. The yarn is then made into sweaters and rugs. People have made clothes from the Samoyed's hair for centuries in Russia, but only recently has this clothing become popular in the United States and Canada.

GOLDEN RETRIEVER

For years a legend has persisted that the Golden Retriever is descended from yellow Russian circus dogs that toured Europe. This is not true. In England in the 1800s, people wanted better hunting dogs. Breeders experimented with various kinds of dogs. One of the breeds they created was a retriever, which, because of the unusual yellow color of its coat, was named the Golden Retriever.

The Golden Retriever proved to be an outstanding hunting dog. But in recent years, it has come to be used as a seeing-eye dog. Seeing-eye dogs literally use their own eyes to guide the blind. Along with other breeds—the German Shepherd, the Labrador Retriever, the Boxer, and the Collie—the Golden Retriever is ideal for guiding the blind. It learns quickly, is even tempered, obedient, and anxious to please its master. During World War I, in Germany, dogs were trained to guide soldiers who had been blinded in battle. It was the first time dogs were trained to guide the blind on a large scale. About fifteen years later The Seeing Eye, a training school for guide dogs, was opened in Morristown, New Jersey.

Seeing-eye dogs must be well trained because people's lives depend upon them. Dogs are carefully chosen for this work by experienced trainers. They talk to the dogs and handle them to see how well they respond to people and if they are alert and

intelligent. Loud noises are made near the dogs, and they are poked when they are not looking. This may seem cruel, but a dog that is easily startled might pull its owner over. On the other hand, a dog that is not alert might not pay attention to its work. Once a dog passes these tests, it is examined by a veterinarian to see if it is healthy. The trainers and veterinarians are so skilled that they seldom choose unsuitable dogs.

When the Golden Retriever is about fourteen months old, it begins four months of training. First the dog learns to wear a harness and to walk with the trainer. Then the trainer pretends to trip over curbs. He makes noises with his feet so that the dog learns not to cross the curb until the trainer says "Forward." The dog is trained to wait for cars to pass before crossing the street.

The trainer also hits trees, poles, low signs, and other obstacles with his hand and teaches the dog to go around them. The trainer says "Right" or "Left" as he and the dog turn, and the dog learns to turn in the correct direction. The dog practices these lessons over and over again. It always knows if what it is doing is right or wrong by the tone of the trainer's voice. The dogs love to be praised; they don't like to be scolded.

After three months of practice the dog is given a final test. The trainer is blindfolded, and he walks around town with the dog. The dog has to prove that it can cross streets correctly, that it can turn right or left, and that it can avoid dangerous places before it can be a seeing-eye dog. Since the dogs are so carefully chosen to begin with, almost all of them pass the test. Those that don't are given additional training.

During the fourth month of training, the dog is assigned to its future owner, and they go to school together. As they work together, the blind person learns what kind of personality the dog has and how best to handle it. The dog learns to take commands from his new owner. Once they feel comfortable together, the blind person and his dog can go home.

The blind person must know the way around his neighborhood so that he can teach his dog where to go when they are out. If they go to the grocery store, the blind person commands his dog to turn right or left at the proper corners. When they have gone to the grocery store often enough, the dog will know how to get there without being told. Sometimes, the blind person has to ask other people for directions if he isn't certain how to get somewhere. He then gives the correct commands to his dog as they walk along.

During their years together, the dog and its blind owner come to depend on each other. The dog guides its owner, and the owner feeds and cares for his dog. Usually they become quite close. When a seeing-eye dog gets old, a younger, more alert dog is brought in to guide its owner. In most cases, the two dogs adjust well to each other, and they live together with the blind person. The older dog can sleep or play while the new dog does all the work.

SAINT BERNARD

Although Saint Bernards lived with people for centuries, many years passed before it was discovered that they had the ability to find lost travelers in the snow. These dogs were first called Talhunds, Alpenhunds, or Barihunds.

The story of the Saint Bernard begins almost two thousand years ago. Large dogs traveled with the Roman army when it marched into the Alps. Three hundred years later, when the Roman army left, the descendants of these dogs remained in the villages and farms and were used as watchdogs and to pull carts.

Centuries later, in A.D. 980, a monk named Father Bernard started a hospice, a place where travelers could get food and rest, in a mountain pass near what is now the Swiss-Italian border. During the 1660s, when outlaws were terrorizing villagers, the monks at the hospice began to use the large dogs as watchdogs. But the monks discovered that the dogs were useful in other ways. Because the dogs could detect a human scent carried on the wind from several miles away, they were able to find travelers lost in the snow. They were especially suited to guiding people along the dangerous paths. They could hear avalanches coming. And they knew how deep the snow was because they could smell the ground.

When someone was lost, the monks sent trained Saint Bernards to search for him. If four dogs were sent, two of the dogs

would lie next to the person to keep him warm. A third dog licked the person's face to keep him awake. The fourth dog ran back for help. When only one dog was sent out, it barked loudly in order to lead rescuers to the missing person.

The method the monks developed for training rescue dogs is similar to that used today. First the trainer hides, and the dog is taught to find him by following his scent. Then the trainer touches a piece of clothing and buries it in the snow; the dog is taught to find it. Finally the trainer and other people bury

themselves in the snow, and the dog tries to find them. Young dogs also learn by accompanying older ones. Saint Bernards do not have to smell anything touched by a lost person in order to find him. They can follow any human scent.

During the 1800s, the reputation of the Saint Bernards for saving lives began to spread around the world. One dog named Barry, who lived between 1800 and 1814, was reported to have saved forty lives. Once while returning to the hospice from a rescue mission, Barry carried a little boy on his back. Barry's fame and the fame of the other rescue dogs gradually increased, and in 1880 these dogs were named for the Hospice of Saint Bernard, which had been named for Father Bernard who had been made a Saint.

Because people wanted a larger, stronger dog that had a better retrieving instinct, the Saint Bernard was crossbred with the Newfoundland in about 1830. As a result of this crossbreeding, the Saint Bernard is one of the largest breeds, often weighing 165 pounds. The heaviest Saint Bernard we know of weighed 295 pounds. The crossbreeding also resulted in two different types of Saint Bernard. One has long hair, the other the more traditional short hair. Snow and ice stick to the long-haired dogs and make them very cold, so only the short-haired dogs are used for rescue work. The long-haired dogs, however, have become very popular as pets and are the type most people are familiar with today. Both short- and long-haired Saint Bernards are white on the chest, feet, and tip of the tail, but the rest of the body is either white with orange or white with shades of red.

About one hundred fifty years ago, an artist named Edwin Landseer painted a picture of a Saint Bernard carrying a keg of cognac around its neck. Many other artists have incorporated this detail in their paintings, but Saint Bernards have never carried kegs around their neck.

Today the Saint Bernard is less often used for rescue work. Most people travel through the mountains in cars and trains. But every year Saint Bernards still save lives near the Hospice of Saint Bernard and elsewhere. Because the Saint Bernard has rescued over twenty-five hundred people over the last three hundred years, it has been named the national dog of Switzerland.

DOBERMAN PINSCHER

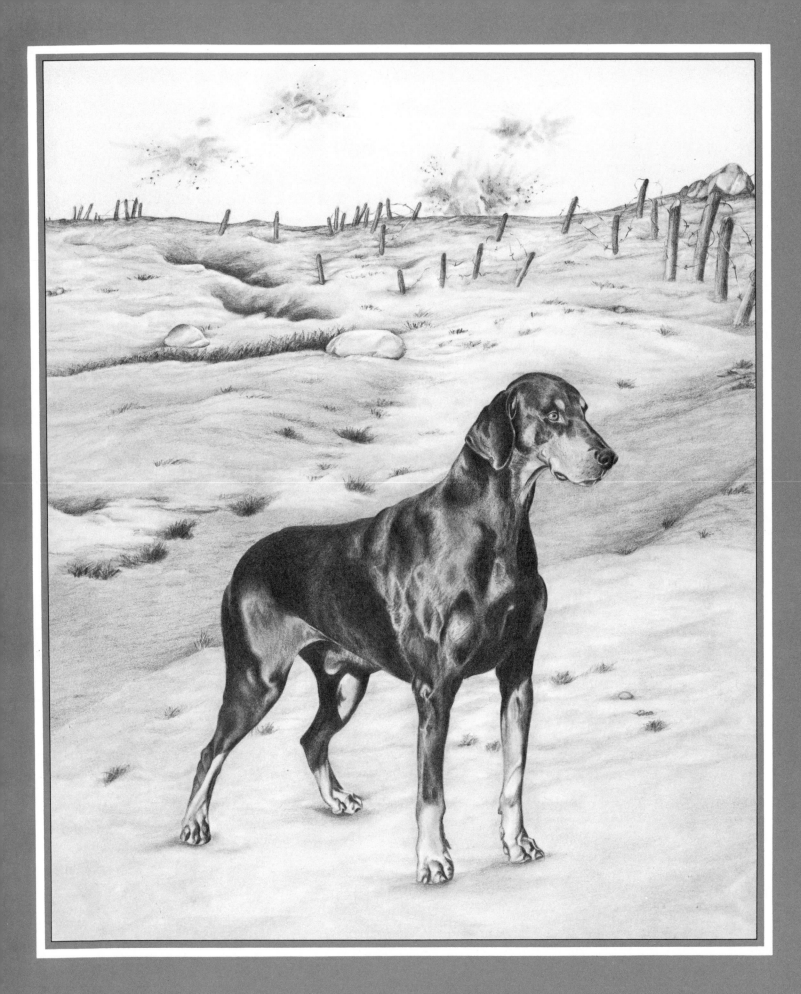

The Doberman Pinscher is often thought of as a dog of war because it has been used by the military. It was originally bred for use as a guard dog by Louis Dobermann, a dogcatcher who lived in Germany at the end of the 1800s. The first Doberman Pinschers were very vicious. In later years, calmer Dobermans were bred, but because of their early reputation, and because they have been used as guard dogs, many people still believe they are mean.

The Doberman Pinscher is a solid, muscular dog that usually weighs about 60 or 70 pounds. Its short coat is either black or reddish brown with tan markings. For the sake of appearance, the Doberman puppy's tail is docked, and its ears are sometimes cropped to make them pointed. Because some people regard this as a cruel practice, many states have made it illegal.

During World War I, seventy thousand Dobermans and other dogs were trained to perform dangerous tasks. Each dog was trained for one purpose, so it would learn its job well. Some Dobermans carried messages around their necks across the battlefield. Other Dobermans were used as ambulance dogs. When a battle ended, a Doberman was sent onto the field with medicine and food tied around its neck for the wounded soldiers. It then ran back to the medics and led them to the wounded men. Some Dobermans were trained to smell poisonous gas and to sniff out buried explosives. Still others were trained to bark at the first

sound of an airplane in order to warn soldiers of an enemy attack.

In World War II Americans donated thousands of dogs to the military. The Marines chose the Doberman Pinscher as their official dog because of its reputation as a guard dog, and they nicknamed it "Devildog." They trained it to use its senses of smell and hearing to find enemy soldiers. They took the dogs out on patrol

on leashes. The dogs were trained to growl softly or to stand perfectly still when they became aware of the enemy in order not to give the Marines' location away. The dogs were also trained to corner enemy soldiers so they would not escape.

After the war, most of the dogs were returned to their owners. But before a dog went home, it had to be retrained. It was important for the dog to learn not to bark and growl at people. To accomplish this, Marines would play with the dog and talk with it gently. To be sure that the dog was ready to go home, it was given a test. Someone would jump at the dog and shout. If the dog did not bark loudly or try to corner the person, it was sent home.

In spite of the skill the Doberman showed during the war, the German Shepherd was chosen as the official dog of the armed forces in 1946. Although the Doberman no longer serves the military, it is often used as a guard dog by private businesses.

BORDER COLLIE

People have used dogs for herding for centuries, and today the Border Collie is the most commonly used sheep dog in English-speaking countries. The Border Collie is probably descended from the Bearded Collie and from other British sheep dogs and hunting dogs. Its name comes from the area where it originated—the border between Scotland and England.

The Border Collie is not to be confused with the Collie most Americans are familiar with. The breed of Collie we know—whose most famous member is the TV and movie dog Lassie—is a Rough coated collie; it is larger than the Border Collie and has longer hair.

The Border Collie weighs between 30 and 50 pounds, and its coat is usually black with small or large amounts of white on the neck, chest, feet, and legs, and on the tip of the tail. Border Collies with short hair work best in warm areas, while those with longer coats are used in cooler climates.

So inborn is the herding instinct of the Border Collie, that Collie puppies often try to herd small animals and even children. The Border Collie is an intelligent dog that learns well from experience. Its training begins at six months and continues for six months after that. The Border Collie's master controls and trains the dog using his voice, whistles, and hand signals. For example, he teaches the dog to turn right by waving his right arm, or by saying "Right," or by giving a certain whistle as the dog turns right. Some dogs are taught to respond to all three types of signals, while others learn only one or two.

The dog practices and practices these commands. When it has been trained, it is able to turn right or left, to run fast or slow, or to stop—all on command. When ordered to "gather," the dog brings the sheep to the master. When told to "drive," it gets the sheep moving. If a sheep is reluctant to move, the dog gives it the "eye"—that is, it crouches down and stalks the sheep while staring straight at it. The sheep doesn't like the dog's action so it

moves. Giving a sheep the "eye" is instinctive behavior that the Collie probably inherited from its hunting ancestors.

The Border Collie can work from sunrise to sunset, day in and day out, with little rest. Even when sheep are grazing

together in one place, the Border Collie runs circles around the flock to keep them from wandering off. If the sheep are standing very close together and the dog wants to get to the other side of the flock in a hurry, it takes a shortcut: it jumps onto their backs and runs across to the other side!

Border Collies are used primarily in the British Isles, Australia, New Zealand, Canada, and the United States. In the vast open spaces of the American West, a single Border Collie can be used to herd as many as one thousand sheep. Border Collies are able to tend sheep without people to direct them. They bark when a stranger or wild animal approaches, and they have even been known to attack wolves or coyotes, which are much larger than they are, in defense of the flock.

While Border Collies are most often used to herd flocks of sheep, they are also trained to work with other livestock. Border Collies are even found on some turkey, duck, and pig farms. Usually Border Collies are trained to work with only one kind of animal so that they will get to know their job very well. While working with cattle, the Border Collie sometimes nips their feet. This doesn't hurt the cattle; it serves to get them moving. But the dog has to be quick because a cow will sometimes try to kick it after being nipped.

AFTERWORD

This book has taken a close look at eleven breeds of dog and the work they have performed. But many other breeds have performed the same work. Besides the Border Collie, the Shetland Sheepdog, the Puli, the Belgian Sheepdog, and the Briard have herded sheep. And the Turnspit, a small, bowlegged dog that can run for hours without stopping, was bred in England to turn cooking spits just as the Bouvier des Flandres did in Belgium. Whatever work needed to be done in a region, there was a particular type of dog suited for the task or that could be bred to do it.

As technology and customs changed, many dogs were no longer needed for the work they were originally intended to perform. Motorized rotisseries and humane animal laws have retired the Bouvier des Flandres and the Turnspit from their endless treadmill running. And the sausage-shaped Dachshund, bred specifically to scamper through tunnels and attack badgers, has been replaced by poisons, traps, and underground electrical fences.

Fortunately, the natural intelligence of dogs and their amazing variety of skills have opened up new areas of work. The Golden Retriever is a perfect example of this. Not only do they continue as fine hunting dogs, but their loyalty and gentleness make them excellent seeing-eye dogs as well.

A similar job shift has occurred in the entertainment industry. For centuries, dogs performed tricks in circuses and at fairs, often riding horses bareback, balancing on their hind legs, or leaping through burning hoops. As movies and television became more popular, these abilities were redirected. Occasionally, a dog such as Lassie or the German Shepherd Rin Tin Tin was featured in his own movie or television series. But because the vast majority of dogs are household pets, most canine actors are seen in one-minute television commercials advertising flea and tick collars or different brands of dog food. Television commercials may not be as glamorous as the movies, but they help increase the popularity of the types of dogs that appear.

Another way in which breeds of dog become popular is through competition in dog shows, Obedience Trials, and Field Trials. Official dog shows with set rules were first held in the middle of the nineteenth century. Each breed is evaluated according to a standard. The standard is what the particular breed should ideally look like and includes general appearance, body structure, shape, size, color, and coat.

Obedience Trials demonstrate how well a dog can be trained to heel or walk next to a master, turn, sit or lie down on command, jump, retrieve, or follow a scent. Field Trials test dogs for the abilities they were initially bred to perform. For instance, in sheep-dog trials, a dog may be commanded to herd sheep into a flock, to separate a sheep from the flock, or drive the sheep into a pen.

Many dogs will maintain the jobs they have traditionally done. No one has invented a mechanical sheep herder to replace the Border Collie, and despite attempts to breed a replacement, the Bloodhound is still the best tracker of scents. What is clear, however, is that the dog's close association with people will continue, and as our way of life changes, so will the work performed by dogs.

INDEX